I've Graduated Now What?

---

4 Steps to Take After College to Find a Job and Start a Life You'll Love

LaTisha Styles

Cover design by Alex Alerrandre

This book is dedicated to every graduating student suddenly thrown into the "real world" having that first *"oh crap!"* moment.

ACKNOWLEDGEMENTS

To my mother and father, thank you for motivating me to reach for the very best and instilling within me a strong work ethic. I am motivated and ambitious because of your dedication and love.

To my husband, thank you for your endless support and honesty during this journey.

To my son, never stop asking why.

Melanie, thank you for your help with this project. I could not have completed it without you.

Kara, thank you for motivating me to complete this book during our mastermind calls. Your help was invaluable.

This Book is For You

This book is for you if you feel stuck and you are ready to get your career started now. That means you want the right job, with the right company, for the right pay.

Lately, the news has been reporting frequently on the millennial generation those born between the years 1981 and 2000. The media personifies millennials as entitled, lazy, self-absorbed, and hopeless when it comes to money habits and career progression. As a millennial myself, I know that we **are** financially literate and we want to work! We just want the right job with the right company.

After graduating from college (twice!) I found myself without a job and deeply discouraged. I sent out multiple resumes, contacted network connections, and worked part-time jobs. Finally, I decided to create my own job and I began writing about what I had learned with my finance degree and what life had taught me about personal finance YoungFinances.com. A few months later, I snagged an entry-level job and worked my way up within the company. This book provides the answers to the same questions I asked, and those questions many recent college graduates ask after graduating.

LaTisha Styles

Do You Have More Questions?

Continue the conversation at
GradNowWhat.com

This page is intentionally blank

Graduating into "The Real World"

188. That is the number of jobs that I applied to during my nearly one year job search. I filled a notebook with job titles and the date that I submitted my resume. I graduated in the middle of The Great Recession and I received few calls for interviews. I had so many hopes and dreams after graduation, but faced rejection after rejection. I have had more experience applying for jobs, writing resumes, and interviewing than I care to admit. I once had six different resumes based on the particular skills I could directly use in those six different types of jobs. I used the 'spaghetti method.' I

am sure you have heard of it. With this method, you throw a handful of spaghetti at a wall and see what sticks. Obviously, you do not want to try this literally, I am speaking metaphorically.

I have also held many jobs; some related to my future career, others that helped me fill the time during my college years. I have worked retail until the wee hours of the morning, setting up a new 'floor set' of clothing trends. Meanwhile, during store hours, I cringed each time a customer dropped a poly blend shirt on the floor; because I knew that either at that moment, or once the store closed, I would be responsible for hanging it back on the rack, buttons secured, zippers zipped.

I once took a job in the food industry thinking that the title of Assistant Manager would save me from grease stains, and the task of asking customers to purchase more by adding fries and a drink. It did not.

I started a part-time job as a guerilla marketer, aggressively approaching strangers and asking them, "Are you in the Loop?" All the while, they stared, puzzled, wondering why this young woman interrupted the conversation.

I also tried a desk job, interning for a top brokerage firm; finally understanding that for a 'desk jockey', cupcake eating contests and occasional pranks were the way to pass the day. As a caretaker, I have worked with children, and adults who act like children.

There were times, towards the end of my college years, when I wished I could go back to being a child. Yes, I enjoyed my freedom as an adult, but after getting rejection after rejection, I wanted no part of the real world.

I started my true career after going back to college for the second time. I had finally learned what I should have done in college the first time around. I learned that I should have joined organizations not for the name but for the networking opportunities. So I decided, after graduating with a Spanish degree and working various odd jobs, that I would go back to school for a Finance degree. This time around, I did things the right way. At least I was sure I had. I got involved in campus activities, I took on an unpaid internship to grow my skill set, and I paired that with a paid internship to take care of my expenses.

After graduating, I thought that I would immediately find a job related to my major. I had the experience, I had the connections, and I had the ambition. One thing that I did not have was a crystal ball. I had no way of knowing that I had chosen an industry that would be so hard hit during the recession. Nevertheless, I kept applying for jobs, I kept tweaking my resume, and I kept reaching out to every contact that I had. In the meantime, I continued to work odd jobs.

Eleven months after I graduated I finally sealed the deal for an entry-level position in finance. I was elated. I had finally made it! However, I still remember how frustrating it feels to transition from the excitement of graduation to the disappointment of unemployment— when you can no longer use the excuse "I'm a student" to justify your income. I want to encourage you if you are feeling stuck. You will not be stuck forever and if you apply the steps in this book, you will be well on your way to achieving success.

Step 1: Write a Job-Getting Resume

Everything is easier said than done. Wanting something is easy. Saying something is easy. The challenge and the reward are in the doing. – Dr. Steve Maraboli

STEP 1: WRITE A JOB-GETTING RESUME

Before you can begin to approach your friends and professional contacts about your job search, you have to polish your resume. If you have not yet created one, then that is your first order of business. As a hiring manager, I have had the task of reviewing resumes and contacting promising candidates for interviews. Most resumes submitted never made it past a preliminary scan. The ones that did make it shared some commonalities that I plan to detail.

I am going to share with you, from my experience, what works. Without holding anything back, you are going to get the details on what to include in your resume, how to format your resume, the key points that you should never forget, and the one tip that will move your resume past round one.

As I was preparing for my first job after graduating college with a finance degree, I created three resumes. They were based upon the three major industries in which I wanted to work. One resume was positioned for a consulting job and emphasized my versatility. I included the different aspects of the jobs I had previously held. I included the consulting work I had done for an organization. I really worked hard to make that resume stand out. The other two were positioned for a job in finance. One was written specifically for the banking side of finance and the other for the investment side of finance. After spending the time and effort on these three resumes, I started chatting with a friend. I must have mentioned the resumes a few times because she asked if I would review her resume and give suggestions. She had an internship opportunity for the corporate office of a major retailer in New York and she wanted to make her resume exceptional. I told her I would be happy to help.

I reviewed her resume, made a few formatting changes, expanded some sections, eliminated a few words, and replaced a few words. I also made keyword changes. These changes were specific to the internship and really helped her resume stand out. Once completed, I gave her quick suggestions so that she would know how to format her resume going forward as her career evolves. After a few weeks she called me. She got the internship! Word quickly spread and I had a few more friends ask for my help. I helped them as well. I used this exact strategy to create my resume. The one that finally landed me a well paying full-time job with a top five investment consulting firm. At the time I was hired, I was delivering sandwiches for a popular chain and I made six dollars an hour plus tips. On a good day I would earn $10-12 per hour. Getting that full-time job immediately doubled my salary and gave me the opportunity to pay off debt and finally get ahead of my budget. I want to help you get the job that will help you get ahead financially as well.

Why You Need a Great Resume

Writing a good resume is the key to landing the job you truly want. However, you not only need a good resume, you need a great one to stand out from the competition. There are many applicants competing for the same job. Perhaps they attended the same college, or graduated from a better school. They may have the same years of experience or more experience. Your resume has to make it to the top of the heap. The latest study by recruiting firm The Ladders shows that hiring managers give each resume no more than a six second scan. Emphasizing your best experience and filling your resume with exactly the right points will allow you to land that job you truly want and deserve to have.

Employers begin reviewing resumes when they start the arduous process of bringing on a new employee. A great resume must showcase your skills, play down any potential weaknesses and really emphasize your strengths. A few years ago, hiring managers would sit and read through each resume before choosing several candidates. But today, the process has changed.

These days, computers scan your resume digitally. For this reason, you need a new set of rules when writing your resume, either as you prepare to get your first job out of college or anytime you are considering switching jobs.

Let's start with the basics. Your resume should tell your story. It should be clear and concise without extra wording and fluff. To accomplish this, it is best to begin with the end in mind. Where do you want to work?

STEP 1: WRITE A JOB-GETTING RESUME

Let's say that you have decided to pursue a job in accounting. You must decide on the type of accounting job you would prefer. Once you have the job narrowed down, think about the top companies where you could work. As you narrow down your choice, you can start to fill in your resume with the most relevant experience. You will also see where your resume might be weak and you can work on getting the necessary experience to fill in any holes.

You might be in panic mode right now if you are a senior in college and you cannot think of career related experience you can add to your resume. Don't worry. I've helped rewrite resumes for people just like you who thought they had no experience. It's still possible to get a job using the skills that you have right now. Presentation is everything and I will show you exactly what to do.

Power Pack Your Resume

We begin with the meat of the resume. Later you will adjust the layout, decide on the proper margins and the perfect font size. As you fill in your experience, you will continue adjusting these elements. Often, the formatting is scheduled as the last item on the resume writing to-do list, but if you format your resume as you write you will be more conscious to only include what is important.

Eliminate Gaps

If there are any gaps in your work history, make sure you fill those gaps. Did you work during the summer while you were in college? Use that experience. Did you participate in extracurricular activities while not working? Include skills that you learned from those activities. For example, time spent as a treasurer in a school club shows that you are active and that you used your college days to practice classroom lessons. Maybe you were laid off recently. What did you do during that time? Did you volunteer? Or did you volunteer your time sitting around the house watching reality shows on TV?

It's important to show a consistent working history because employers want to know that you are 'employable'. This means that they do not want to hire you if no one else wants to hire you. It's sort of frustrating but that is how it works. If you have too many gaps, the employer may think that you are a job hopper.

I worked several jobs while in college and some concurrently. On my resume, I included most of the jobs but eliminated any that were not necessary to show a continuous flow of jobs. I also used skills that I learned from extracurricular activities to fill in gaps in my work experience.

Emphasize Skills

Think about achievements that make you stand out as a candidate. An all-star baseball championship may not be appropriate in the work section of the resume, but you can include it in a section along with skills and achievements. The choice of what to include depends on what you want the employer to know most about you.

Does your work ethic show through your grades? Add your class rank. Do you have exceptional social talents? Include school clubs and leadership awards. This section delivers the message that you are the very best candidate. To emphasize your hard earned skills, use a "top achievements" section. This section emphasizes 3 to 5 skills or achievements. Take a moment to write down your top skills and achievements.

TOP SKILLS

Bonus

Use an odd number of achievements in this section. Why? According to the 'Rule of Odds', an odd number of items is more pleasing to the human eye. Sound crazy? Pay attention to the next sitcom or commercial that you watch and you will see this rule in action. A typical shot will have one person or three people. Odd numbers are preferred and used often.

Elaborate on Strengths

A great resume will elaborate on your strengths. Having a hard time determining your strengths? At this point it would be good to start asking past employers, friends, and family. What strengths do they notice in you? What strengths do you notice in yourself? Be honest with yourself. What traits would you like to have? Write down those strengths and weaknesses in the following box.

STRENGTHS	WEAKNESSES

I find that it helps to ask new friends for their first opinion of you. Don't take offense if their first impression was not favorable. You are asking so you can improve. Trust me, when you are in an interview you will likely not get this precious feedback; so accept it graciously when you do get it from the people that matter.

Next, highlight at least three of your top strengths. Are you a good leader? Think about the experience where you had to lead. Are you creative? Do you think well on your feet? If so, you should have numerous examples to cite on your resume and more in your interview as well.

Use This Simple Tip To Get Ahead of the Competition

If you only made one simple change to your resume, this next tip would be it. Even if you forget the margins and forget the layout, focus on this one simple tip to help you get the job.

Never Passive, Always Active.

Your resume should read as if you are the star of the show. If you remember grammar class, the passive voice reads as if the subject is the recipient of the action. The active voice shows the subject as the creator of the action. Nothing in your career should be happening to you; you should be the one actively making your career happen. Use the best wording in your resume to demonstrate this for you. Take a look at this example and to see the passive and active voice in use.

Example 1: Was elected president of the Business Leaders Club.

Example 2: Ran a successful campaign and won the title of President of the Business Leaders Club.

Think about it. Who would you rather hire? The person who just happened to fall into the position of president because an election went well or the person who actively persuaded people to vote for them? The first is a passive voice. The second shows more action and more ambition. Use action verbs in your resume and the descriptions under each position.

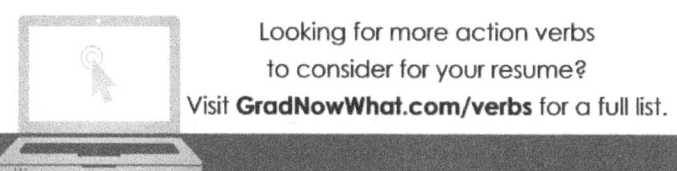

Looking for more action verbs
to consider for your resume?
Visit **GradNowWhat.com/verbs** for a full list.

Focus on These Top Eye-Catching Elements

Choose the Right Layout

There is no single specific way to craft a resume. The proper layout depends on what is acceptable in your industry. For example, if you were looking for a position as an actor, a call sheet with photos would be your resume. If you are searching for a position in the design industry, a more creative resume is fine. In the business world, a standard one-page resume is typical.

Choose the layout that fits the position for which you apply. The layout includes the number of pages, the photo on the front, if any, and allowable colors. A simple search on the web will help determine the correct format. For example, search "sample resumes for Junior Accountant" and you will find a few resume samples. Scan through these to get an idea of the typical resume layout for the industry.

You may be tempted to make your layout eye-catching and different, right? Bad idea. At this stage of the game, the idea is to show the hiring manager that you know what your industry expects. You don't want to submit a three-page resume to a hiring manager in the business world of standard one-page resumes. I can almost guarantee that they will not look past the first page. There are other ways to make your resume stand out. Here are the most important elements.

Use White Space and Margins

White space and margins are the first eye-catching elements that you can adjust to make your resume stand out. Proper use is important. Use too much white space and you look inexperienced. Use too little white space and your resume becomes an eyesore and a headache to read.

I'm sure that you could squeeze plenty of accomplishments into your resume. Between education, internships, study abroad programs, and languages; your resume could easily span 2 to 3 pages. In some cases, a two page resume is acceptable, for example; a resume that requires explanations for each position. However, you must present your information in a concise manner. Avoid writing extensively about your professional history. Save that for the online professional profile, which I will discuss later.

Align dates, cities, and job titles. Write your resume so that the eye naturally flows from left to right, and back easily without getting bogged down in any one place. Use bullet points when needed. The key is to use the white space to your advantage so that the eye flows naturally from one line to the next. You want the hiring manager to notice the key information and good use of white space can help tremendously.

The margin is the white space around the edges of your resume. Margins are your friend and should be used with care. On my resume, I used half-inch margins on the left and right sides as well as the top and one inch at the bottom.

A general rule of thumb is to give enough space for a thumb. I like to call this the Thumb-Rule. Try it. Pick up a sheet of printer paper in one hand as if you were reading it. Do you see how your thumb covers the outside inch or so? Ideally, when your resume is being read by hand, the recruiter shouldn't have to move her thumb to read your experience.

Select the Best Font

The choice of font is not as important as the choice of margin space, but it does deserve some attention. Typical font choices are Times New Roman, Arial or Verdana. Choose one of these three fonts for a standard resume. For more of a creative flair, try Garamond or Georgia. Beyond that I do not recommend other fonts. Keep in mind that your resume format should be simple and easy to read.

The selected font size will help fit all of your content in the desired space. If your accomplishments are spilling into the next page, a smaller font size can certainly make a difference. However, do not reduce the font size drastically. Ideally, the font should be no smaller than 11pt font. 12pt font is preferable. Feel free to increase to 13pt or 14pt if you are lacking information on your resume.

Why Your Resume Fails to Pass Round One

Now you have your physical resume that you can attach to job applications and mail out as needed, but you also need to know how the new online resume systems function. It all comes down to one word, or several, if you will, keywords.

You've Failed to Use Keywords

Computers scanning resumes online are searching for certain words. These words are key phrases that are popular in the industry and signal to the computer that your resume is relevant. Each set of keywords that you use is specific to your industry and possibly even the job.

For example, in college I joined the student managed investment fund. We researched stocks and recommended purchases for the investment portfolio. In the industry, this is called buy-side analysis. So instead of saying that I 'researched stocks and recommended purchases', I simply wrote, "performed buy-side analysis with the student managed investment fund." Immediately, when the computer scans and recognizes this industry keyword, my resume is scored higher than another candidate's resume that only mentioned the words stock research.

You should know your industry well enough to know what the 'buzz words' are. Use these words throughout your resume. If you are not quite sure what buzz words to use, pick up a journal or industry publication. You will recognize what words repeat often and begin to see a pattern.

Typing keywords in the margins in white font is an additional suggestion so the computer reads them but the eye cannot. That is an option if you are aiming to squeeze in more keywords. However, you can fit them naturally into your resume just as well.

Looking for industry keyword suggestions?
Visit **GradNowWhat.com/keywords**
and get a listing of top keywords to
use for the most popular jobs.

You Forgot to Update Professional Profiles

Your resume does not stop with the physical or online application; the resume check often extends to the Internet. Are you checking your online profiles and what you share publicly? A recent study conducted by Harris Interactive for CareerBuilder.com, showed that 43 percent of employers are using social networks to screen job candidates. Of those employers that check social networks, 51 percent found content that caused them to not hire the candidate.

In that survey 46 percent of employers mentioned they rejected a candidate because the candidate posted provocative or inappropriate photographs or information.

Forty-one percent decided to reject a candidate because the candidate posted content about them drinking or using drugs. But in the same way that your personal information on social networks can be harmful, you can also use it to your advantage.

Begin to set up your online footprint. At the very least, create a LinkedIn profile with professional achievements. There is one section of LinkedIn that is easily overlooked: the recommendations section. Ask for a recommendation from anyone with whom you have worked, preferably former managers, and industry peers. Your resume may only be one page, but your LinkedIn profile can extend with further information that supports you as the top candidate.

In the same study by Harris Interactive, after screening the candidate online, 46 percent decided to hire in part because they thought the profile provided a good feel for the candidate's personality and fit. While 45 percent of those surveyed chose to hire because they thought the profile supported the candidate's professional qualifications. Use professional profiles to your advantage and hide the information that does not cast you in the best light.

In its infancy, Facebook was intended for college students only. After a weekend out, friends would relive the night with photos they posted and shared. The tagging feature allows almost anyone to tag your name to a picture you might not want others to see. Instead, update your privacy settings so that you approve all tag requests in photos in which you are tagged. If you plan to keep your Facebook account active while you search for jobs, I recommend at least inactivating this tagging feature. I have friends that closed their Facebook accounts while they were job searching. This may be easier for you than cleaning up the entire profile.

The key is to maintain a digital footprint but manage the information that could surface. It's all about presenting your best self to the employer. You can grow your personal brand and present a positive image of yourself on your social networks. Start by sharing articles from your industry and commenting on status updates from journalists that write about topics concerning your industry.

You're Not Leveraging LinkedIn

Your LinkedIn profile is one of the first places that a potential employer can see your digital footprint.

LinkedIn is a professional social networking site where you can highlight your talents and experience. However, if used incorrectly, your LinkedIn profile can repel potential employers and recruiters. I will start with six important features that you should take advantage of on LinkedIn and finish with how to leverage LinkedIn so recruiters come to you.

LinkedIn Picture

Use a quality photo of yourself in professional dress. A blue or white button down top is common. A suit jacket is appropriate but not necessary depending on your industry. Snap one yourself using a stable surface and a timer or simply have a friend take one for you.

Use a non-distracting background so that you remain the focus of the photo.

LinkedIn Title

Your LinkedIn title describes your job title or if you are unemployed, the title you would like. Avoid the use of unemployed as a title.

If you are looking for a job as an investment analyst for example, an appropriate title could be 'Investment Analyst seeking the right opportunity' or 'Recent graduate seeking Investment Analyst position.'

Your title could also include your strengths and read something like this, "Motivated, driven, results oriented analyst seeking the right opportunity." That may be too many adjectives, but you get the idea.

LinkedIn Description

The description section is where you can really flex some muscle. Feel free to write in the first person. This section is similar to a cover letter. It should reiterate your strengths and elaborate on them as well.

If you describe yourself as detail-oriented, then give an example of when this strength helped a previous employer. Be descriptive! Most job titles don't explain what you actually did in that position.

Only write in third person when your accomplishments speak for themselves. If you are considered a public figure, recognized speaker, or industry expert, then a description written in the third person is acceptable. However, the entire point of a social network is to be social and approachable. Writing in the first person certainly makes you more approachable.

LinkedIn Keywords

The World Wide Web is a vast place and searching for exactly what you need requires a bit of skill, that is, unless you know exactly what words to use. The same way that Google and Bing are search engines, LinkedIn is a search engine. LinkedIn allows a recruiter to quickly and easily find candidates for open positions.

In order to maximize your chances of being found on LinkedIn via search, you have to use the appropriate keywords. Start searching for others that are in your field or that hold your dream job. Pull together a list of keywords and phrases then use these words in your profile. Include them in your description and title if possible. Now the recruiter can find you that much easier.

LinkedIn Recommendations

Getting solid recommendations is one of the best ways to power pack your LinkedIn profile. Ask for recommendations from classmates if you worked on large projects together. Seek recommendations from mentors and current employers. The key is to get at least three solid recommendations from trusted professionals. Your profile will really shine.

LinkedIn Endorsements

Endorsements go hand in hand with recommendations and they make it easy to find candidates based on keywords as well. When you include marketing as a keyword in your profile for example, LinkedIn will automatically ask your connections if you know about marketing.

This is a one-click yes or no option.

The more connections that endorse you for marketing, the higher you will rank in the LinkedIn search for that keyword. To get endorsements, ask or simply endorse others. They will likely reciprocate.

Connecting on LinkedIn

Classmates

Now that your profile is complete, it is time to connect. Start with your classmates. Add each classmate that you can find. As you both grow professionally, your connections will grow even stronger. For example, I added a classmate and friend from a student group and now he is a hedge fund manager. We have both grown professionally and it makes our network stronger.

Professors

Add your professors as well, and don't forget department heads and connections from student group advisors. Your goal is to connect with as many professionals as possible.

Family friends

Once you've added your classmates and professors, add your family friends. Tell them you are searching for a job to start your career. I was able to secure a few interviews this way. It never hurts to ask.

LinkedIn can be your best friend if you use the social network properly. Start by cleaning up your profile and optimizing it so you can jump-start your career.

Now you are ready to get out there and get that job! You have what it takes to be the one hired. You can do it. These tips will propel you to the front of the pack. But this information does nothing if you do not take action! The first step is to set aside time in your day to look at your resume and highlight the best stuff. Now rework it based on what you've learned here and get to work!

Step 2: Locate a Job in Your Career Field

Life is short. Work somewhere awesome.

I had a full strategy when I first started applying for jobs. First, I created a job search notebook. I listed the top firms that I would consider and then I added second tier firms as well. Each time I sent off an application I wrote down the date and the job title. Then I created another list of all of the people that I knew that had a job in the finance industry. I contacted each of them either calling or messaging on LinkedIn, depending on the strength of the connection. I set up a meeting with the head of the finance department at my college and spoke to him about my career goals. I understand what it takes to find that perfect job. The job that you have been thinking about while you studied for your final exams. When you do not have a job lined up, it may seem that all of the good jobs are taken. Not to worry, there are a few simple ways that you can find that perfect career position. It all comes down to one activity.

Networking.

What is Networking?

College students often dread networking. When I first heard the term, I thought it was ridiculous. Why should I become friends with someone just for what they could offer me? I don't like to be taken advantage of, and I wouldn't want to do that to someone else.

Once I graduated from college the first time with a Spanish degree, I realized that I should have networked more. I would ask friends and fellow graduates, "how did you get that job?" I always heard the same thing. "A friend of mine told me about it." How did they have friends that I didn't have? Where could I find these friends with all of the connections? It took me a while but I finally realized that these so-called friends that knew about all of the jobs were really just acquaintances to my friends. I made it my mission to learn to network and meet the right friends.

You don't have to be a leech to build a great network. The first thing I think of when I meet someone new is how can I help them? By thinking of a way to help them first, I am shifting the focus from myself. This allows me to be more approachable and friendly. Most people can sniff out a 'user' from a mile away. When I notice that someone only wants to talk with me because of what I can offer him or her, I generally shy away. However, in order to build your net worth, it is important to have a few key people in your network.

Network in Person

Visit the College Career Center

Stop by your college career center. The career center is connected with local organizations that want you! Those businesses contact the career center on a regular basis to offer open positions specifically for graduating college students.

Call, Email, or Meet your Professors

Using this one technique, I landed an interview with a company that I never would have considered. There are companies that specifically ask professors and department heads for top talent. If you were smart enough to become friends with your professors or if you were memorable in some other positive way then you should make it a point to contact them for help. Call or email and tell them you are still looking for a position.

Join an Industry Specific Organization

I used this technique to get an informational interview with a young woman who works in my field. An informational interview is an informal conversation with someone in your industry that can give you the inside scoop on what actually happens day-to-day. When you meet people in your industry use informational interviews to continue to learn about your field, then you will find more and more opportunities. Make sure you have some personal business cards printed up. Focus on meeting 1 to 3 people at each function. Then follow up for an informational interview. Don't feel pressured that you have to meet everyone at the function. It will make it easier for you to make a meaningful connection with those that you do meet and keep in touch.

Go to Student Functions as an Alumnus

If you were a member of a student organization as an undergraduate then you should remember the special members-only functions. You will likely be able to continue attending those functions as an alumnus. At those functions be sure to chat with fellow alumni— sometimes you can get a tip for an open position in their company.

Network Online

Just searching, applying, and attending interviews while looking for your first career position directly after college can be a full-time job all by itself. I remember searching for my first job. I used to get frustrated when I saw former classmates hired by friends. It made me think that all of the work I did to earn good grades was for nothing.

However, getting good grades is only half of the battle when it comes to finding a job. Whom you know is the other half of the battle. In addition, it can be the most important part of the battle. Networking in person can help you find jobs before they are listed online. But what if you see a job online and you do not have the connections? You will need to begin networking online. Use these tips to make the process easier and leverage your networks.

Use Multiple Job Search Engines

Do not be afraid to use more than one search engine to find a job. You may think that open positions are on all of the large sites but that is not entirely true. Try Monster.com AND CareerBuilder.com. Test out Indeed.com and look for positions directly on company websites. After you have checked these sources, try an industry specific job search engine. For example, in finance, you can search OneWire.com for entry-level and more advanced financial positions. The site also has a networking option so candidates can meet potential employers.

Get the ultimate list of
job search websites at
GradNowWhat.com/jobs

LinkedIn is a great place to look for a job because it already includes the element of professional networking. The job search feature is limited to jobs that might interest you. However, if you perform a search using the right keywords, you may find other jobs. The ability to connect directly with the recruiter is a major advantage to job searching on LinkedIn.

Get Noticed For Your Skills

Before you start reaching out, it is important that you update your resume and write a cover letter for your job search. You may receive an immediate request and you should be ready. Take the time to clean up your social networks and remove any potentially embarrassing material. You want a potential employer to notice you for your skills, not your ability to do a keg stand. Update your LinkedIn profile and ask your close connections and previous employers for recommendations and endorsements. Highlight relevant work history, skills and professional memberships.

You can also stand out by creating a blog or a one-page online resume. Create a blog to talk about your experience, your industry, and explore topics that interest you. A one-page resume is similar to a LinkedIn profile but you can customize it more to match your specific skills. If you are in the design or creative field, you can create an online portfolio and stand out as a candidate.

Connect Online Via Professional Networking

Recruiters are always on the hunt for solid candidates. Take the time to find and connect with recruiters in your industry. Then, add all of your professional connections on LinkedIn. Start to share updates on interesting articles that you have read and stay active on a weekly basis. Join a group dedicated to your industry and chat with those members.

Once you start making meaningful connections, take it a step further. Ask for an in person meeting or Skype chat. Before the meeting, prepare some questions that you can ask. This is not a formal interview but a conversation. Your goal is simply to create a deeper connection with an online friend.

Networking online is very similar to networking in person. You meet a new connection, find out how you can help them and discuss how they may be able to help you. Then you continue the conversation and look for ways to add value going forward.

Step 3: Ace That Interview

Job interviews are like first dates. Good impressions count. Awkwardness can occur. Outcomes are unpredictable.

Participating in mock interviews at the college career center was one of the best things I have ever done. A mock interview gives you an opportunity to practice a full interview and fine-tune your interview skills. There are small changes you can make to improve your prospects. I learned that I look up to the ceiling or off to the side when answering questions. That habit could make me seem untrustworthy. I learned to look the interviewer in the eye and maintain comfortable eye contact. At first, I practiced by staring at a spot in between the eyes, then I moved on to making direct eye contact and looking away less often. Eventually, as my confidence grew, I sustained comfortable eye contact. Other small changes drastically improved my interviewing skills.

An interview is your opportunity to shine or to crash and burn. You have to be ready to answer the questions and present yourself as the best candidate for the position to be hired. It is easy to make mistakes and lose a position because you said the wrong thing. To help you make the best first impression, here are five interview tips you won't want to forget.

Prepare with a Pre-Interview

Prepare by pre-interviewing with potential questions. For example, there are some questions that you are almost guaranteed to hear during your interview. Questions like "Tell me about yourself" or "What is your greatest weakness?" and the best one, "Why should we hire you?" These are questions that you should expect to hear on your interview. Practice your answers or jot down a few bulleted ideas so you can answer naturally.

You can also research questions that are typical for your specific industry. If you are interviewing for a job in finance, healthcare, or marketing; there are certain questions that determine your skill set. Be ready to answer those questions by preparing responses in advance.

Research in Advance

Next, research the company. Find out everything you can about the company. Who are they and what do they do? Is the company publicly traded? If so, you can find news or recent events directly on the investor relations website. This information can give you insight on what the company does best and any recent events of note.

If the company is private you could also research their website. You might have to do a little more digging or do some searches online. Look for employees on LinkedIn that you may be able to contact for an informational interview. Try to discover what you can, so that you can ask an intelligent question about the company and not something that is obvious and easily found on their website.

You want to be very prepared and part of that is researching the company and finding out what they do and how you, as their future employee, fit into the company's growth plans. Doing your research is going to help you during the interview when you have to ask questions. Typically, at the end of the interview, the interviewer will ask if you have any questions for them. At this time you may ask a question about the interviewer, or how the position that you're interviewing for fits in with the company, or what could be done to improve on the position. Ask if there is anything that they think you could do to go above and beyond. Ask what the day-to-day is like. This is where you really want to impress the employer by asking very specific, direct questions. If you do not ask a question, the interviewer could get the impression that you are not interested or worse, that you are unintelligent.

Top 10 Most Common Interview Questions

As you start the process of finding, interviewing for, and landing your first entry-level job, you might feel a bit apprehensive. I know I felt that way.

As a type-A personality, I like to be prepared. I want to know exactly what I should expect and when to expect it. With this in mind, I set off to research as much as I could about landing my first job.

I found that I could expect a few of the same typical questions. These are the questions that I have laid out below along with suggestions on how to answer.

As a unique candidate, your answer will be different than the answer of the next candidate simply because you have different life experiences.

1) Tell me about yourself.

This question presents an opportunity for you to give your elevator pitch. Don't give your life story. I remember an interview where I started talking about my childhood. I saw an odd look from the interviewer. I quickly sped up to my professional story. Stick to personal and professional accomplishments that directly relate to the position for which you are applying.

2) What are your strengths?

This question is also an opportunity to emphasize your key selling points. Prepare to provide examples for each strength as well. But get ready for what is coming next...

3) What are your weaknesses?

Use this question as an opportunity to show personal growth. You can throw in an old weakness and how you've developed professionally. Or, you can use a strength disguised as a weakness. My favorite one goes something like this, "I have a hard time sharing responsibility. I always like to see a project to the end." I have a few that I alternate but I always have at least one weakness prepared.

4) What motivates you?

Your answer to this question helps the interviewer decide how well you will do in the company. If you are motivated by praise, for example, then they know how to squeeze that extra productivity out of you.

5) Tell me about a time you experienced ___. What did you do?

It may be a bit more difficult to prepare for this question. You'll have to think on your feet. They may ask you for a time that you had to struggle, or a time that you had to deal with a lazy coworker. If you can't think of something, use an experience from college. They will understand. Most importantly, you have to show that you have experience dealing with tough situations.

6) Where do you see yourself in 5 years?

You should discuss that you see yourself growing with the company. Even if you think that you will likely leave in a few years for a higher salary, don't say it. Make sure they know that you are willing to stay for the right opportunity.

7) Why did you leave your previous job?

You might think this is an opportunity to bash your previous employer but it is not. That is in poor taste. Instead, discuss your goals and how you wanted to stretch yourself and reach for a better opportunity. Do not discuss pay or interpersonal conflict as a reason for leaving your previous job.

8) Why do you want to work for us?

"Because I want to get paid." Sorry but the logical answer is not the proper answer. Demonstrate your desire to work for this company in particular. Maybe you appreciate how they do business. If so, talk about that. Keep it short but powerful.

9) Why should we hire you?

You are not the only candidate. You have to show that you are the best one for the job. Emphasize your skills and play down any concerns that the interviewer has brought up. This is the time to sell yourself and your capabilities. You want to be remembered as the best option.

10) Do you have any questions for us?

Why, yes I do. Always. You should have at least 3 questions prepared. Ask about the interviewer. You could ask why they like the company. Ask about the company and its goals. And finally ask about the position. When they expect to fill it, if they see you as a good fit. Leave on a high note and after the final questions; thank the interviewer for their time.

Dress for Success

Dress the part. When going on an interview, you always want to look your best. I once heard that you don't dress for the job you have, you dress for the job that you want. And sometimes even nicer than the job you want. Even if you are interviewing for a job at a restaurant, where you might wear jeans everyday as your uniform, you still should wear nice slacks or a skirt and a nice top for the interview.

Depending on the industry you may have to wear something a little bit more formal. For example, if you are interviewing for a position in finance, wear black or dark blue. Dress in a suit with pinstripes or plain colors. In addition, keep your hair pulled back if it falls past your shoulders. You need to appear very conservative for a job in finance when you are interviewing.

If you are interviewing for a job in marketing or with a start-up you may have a bit more flexibility. For example, you can wear a green suit or a dark green color. It doesn't just have to be black or blue; you can get away with a pop of color. A pink or teal colored accent item like a pocket square handkerchief will work or for ladies, a nice colorful top to go underneath your shirt. Regardless, you always want to make sure that you are dressing the part and that you are projecting that image of you on the job and working. Show them how you would present yourself if you started work the very next day. That helps the hiring manager visualize you in the position from the first impression.

Arrive On Time

You must be on time. There's a very simple quote about the importance of being on time.

If you're early, you're on time. If you're on time, you're late. If you're late, don't even bother showing.

It is important to be on time. Your first meeting is the first impression for the employer. If you are not on time then they will likely have a negative impression of you before even meeting you.

Are you perpetually late? You are not alone. Many of us, myself included, have a hard time with punctuality every now and again. Here are ways to prevent being late.

> 1. Scout out the area beforehand. If you are not familiar with where you are

going and the building where you will be interviewing, then check out the area.

2. Plan a test trip to gauge traffic. Be prepared for your interview so that when you arrive there are no surprises. Plan for extra time if you are taking public transportation.

3. Early is better than late. You should be at least 15 minutes early. That is a good rule of thumb.

4. Prepare the night before. Select your clothes and make sure you have gas in your car. Those last minute stops add up.

Follow Up

After the interview, you can either send an e-mail or a physical letter depending on how quickly they are expecting to fill the position. During the interview you should have asked, "When are you looking to fill this position?" Once you have the answer, you know whether they are looking to fill the position immediately or if they have some time. To follow up, get the e-mail address of the interviewer. Send them an e-mail right away, either that day or that afternoon. You can write something like this.

Hello Mr./Mrs./Ms. LAST NAME,

Thank you for taking the time to meet with me. I remember that you mentioned that you were looking for _____ and I am confident that my experience _____ makes me the perfect candidate for the position. I look forward to hearing from you.

Best regards,

In this short letter, you want to reiterate your competitive advantages to reinforce why you are the best candidate and why they should hire you. Write concisely in just a few sentences. If you discussed something in the interview that required a follow-up, for example, if they had a question about your references that you couldn't answer at the time, then the e-mail follow-up is a great time to do it.

Follow up! It really does make a difference. You can mail a physical letter as well. Physical letters are not as common so if you have a chance, put that in the mailbox the next day. That is going to position you beyond the other candidates that did not put in as much effort.

Remember, finding the right career position is about the right fit for you and the employer, so don't sell yourself short! Remember the little things that may help you get the job.

Bonus: Phone Interview Tips

Typically, before you have an in-person interview, you're likely to have a phone interview.

This will be important, because this will be the first of the first impressions that you make with your potential new employer. Here are tips for successful phone interviews.

Prepare

Prepare the same way that you would for an in-person interview. This means researching the company, preparing questions that you know you're likely to be asked, and being ready for any behavioral type or industry specific questions that may come your way.

Watch Yourself

Use a mirror for posture and facial expressions. I use a mirror when I record instructional videos so I remember to smile while I am recording. This is a technique I am confident will help you be successful in your phone interview. Smile and sit up straight. It's going to help you breathe better so that your words flow better, and so you will not stumble over them.

Stay Focused

Minimize noise and distractions. When you're having a phone interview you are likely taking the call in your house but it is possible there are distractions in the background. Children, slamming apartment doors, or the neighbor's barking dogs could create a distracting environment. Give yourself a very quiet area for your interview. The last thing you want is for the interviewer to have the idea in his or her mind that your life is hectic. If they perceive that your life is chaos, then they might think that you will bring that chaos into their company, which is exactly what they do not want.

The only thing that you can give on a phone interview is your perception. That's the brightness of your voice. That is the silence in the background, and that is your great interviewing because you are prepared for the interview.

Step 4: Spend and Save Your First Paycheck

The time to prepare for any emergency – and certainly the loss of a paycheck – is before it happens.

The moment I walked into the building for the in-person interview, I knew that it was time to show what I had to offer. A few days later, when I got the phone call with the job offer I was so excited. As a recent graduate with a finance degree, I had already created a spreadsheet with three salary scenarios. The first scenario included the bare minimum salary that I was willing to accept so I could cover my expenses. The second scenario allowed me to cover expenses and put extra on the debt I had accumulated in the past few years. Finally, the third scenario allowed me to do all of that and move into my own apartment. I waited silently on the phone as I listened to the offer details.

I heard great news. My best-case scenario salary was within reach! I immediately started planning my budget now that I had a specific salary number.

Then I did a happy dance.

When you lock in that first salary, there are a few items to handle in order to get started on the right financial footing.

Take Advantage of Free Retirement Money

First, determine if your company has a company match program for retirement. There are retirement options where the company will match your contributions to an employer-sponsored plan.

The match might be dollar for dollar for every dollar that you contribute up to the first three percent of your salary. In order to claim your free money, designate three percent of your salary to contribute to your company sponsored retirement plan. That is an immediate return on your investment and gives you a head start into retirement savings.

Save for Emergencies

Think of that contribution as long-term savings that you will not get to use until retirement. If that is the case, you need emergency savings. Set a goal to save at least ten percent of your take home pay. That is a principle that I learned from the book The Richest Man in Babylon and it has helped me tremendously.

That is the simplest way to budget. Start with your savings and then enjoy yourself.

Spend some money. You've earned it.

It's all about balance. It's all about what you want to do and what your personal financial goals are.

Create Your First Budget

If you have ambitious goals then it is time to create a budget for the remaining income. When I started my job, I knew that I wanted to pay off debt within three years so I created a budget. There are many ways to create a budget but this one is very simple. It is the envelope budget. The envelope method is a great method if you are having a hard time figuring out how to budget. It is like a baby budget starter method. It is perfect for beginners and it is easy to budget with this method.

How to Budget with the Envelope Method

You will need envelopes, a marker, and your cash. Either you receive your paycheck by direct deposit or you go to the bank and deposit it. Once you deposit your check, figure out what automated transactions you have coming out. Leave enough cash in your bank account for any automated bill pay.

For example, if you have a $50 cell phone bill paid by direct draft, then leave that amount in your account. Withdraw everything else as cash.

Let's say that you get paid $1,000 each week and you have $500 worth of bills to pay that you can pay online. I recommend keeping the $500 plus about 10% as a buffer. That's $550 each week in your account. I always suggest having a small buffer of cash in your checking account. One unexpected expense or error can cause an overdraft. Then, withdraw the remaining $450.

Create Envelope Categories

Now it is time to think of your envelope categories. Set aside an envelope for each budget category. You may decide that you want an envelope for entertainment, one for travel, and one for groceries and personal supplies. You can choose as many budget categories as you like but try to keep five or fewer for simplicity. Write the title of the budget category on each of your envelopes.

Determine Your Spending

Determine how much you plan to spend in each budget category. You can choose an even split where each budget category gets the same amount of money. Or, you can choose a split based on level of importance. Remember to be honest with yourself. It's your budget. You have the power to change it if you want.

Fill Your Envelopes

Now, fill your envelopes with cash based on the spending you have determined for each budget category. When an entertainment expense comes up, you can pull money directly from the entertainment envelope. When that envelope is empty, you are done with entertainment until your next paycheck.

Graduate to a Stronger Budget

While the envelope budget is a great way to start, there is room for failure. Moving cash between envelopes to fit your wants can cause a budget breakdown. Instead, graduate to a stronger budget. Using the same budget categories, set up sub accounts within your checking account, and transfer the cash within your account. Pay yourself first by saving, your bills next using automatic bill pay, and feel comfortable spending the remainder. If you have more goals then increase your savings percentage.

Creating a simple but manageable budget that you can stick to will help you on your journey to financial success.

The Final Key to Getting Unstuck

Alone, this book can do nothing to pull you out of your rut. Ultimately, it is up to you to change your life. Begin by taking action on what you have read. Start with one section at a time and you will create your success.

I believe that if you take the time to apply what you have read, you WILL get that job that you desire. When you do, send me a message at **GradNowWhat.com/success** so I can feature your success on the site. Your story will motivate others to take action.

Do you need more hands-on help? Visit **GradNowWhat.com/resume** to schedule a resume review.

I started my career with no connections, and I graduated from a small college in Georgia. I paid for college on my own without help from my parents and I was the first one in my immediate family to graduate with a degree. I would not allow anything to hold me back and I want you to do the same.

I believe in you and I know that you are truly capable of success. If I can do it, there is nothing stopping you. I wish you the best on your journey to success.

www.ingramcontent.com/pod-product-compliance
Lightning Source LLC
Chambersburg PA
CBHW070831180526
45168CB00002B/801